Understanding AI:
Uncommon Insights for the Busy Learner

Dr. Sandeep Krishnamurthy
dr.sandeep.krishnamurthy@gmail.com
https://www.linkedin.com/in/sandeepk1/

WHY THIS BOOK MATTERS

AI has transformed our world. However, for many learners, there are some gaps in their knowledge of what has already happened and will continue to happen.

My goal is to reduce your confusion and provide a clear idea of what AI really is and how it is transforming our world. In a sea of contrasting and misleading information, I believe that this will be very helpful in understanding what is true and how it matters.

I seek to clarify and explain the most important ideas. This book can be used in a wide variety of university and high school classes as a supplement. It is really a quick read- but each time you re-read it, you will find something new and insightful to ponder. In this way, I hope this book becomes your companion.

You will find the writing style to be terse- that is because I am trying really hard to distill what I think is important and bring it to you. Simply lengthening the content really does not help- you can always feed it into your favorite AI and get a longer version.

Before you start reading, I suggest you do the following to catch up on the current state of AI (most are free)-

1. Locate GoogleLM and convert a PDF file of your choice to a podcast. (Remember to not include any personally identifiable information when you do this.)
2. Use Microsoft Co-Pilot to reply to an email message or create a summary of a Teams audio call.
3. Try Reclaim.AI to understand how you could schedule using an AI assistant.
4. Visit the website of Ruben Hassad to get a masterclass in prompt engineering- https://www.rubenhassid.ai/

Happy learning!

AI FUNDAMENTALS

Chapter 1: Generative AI is Not the Entire Story
Chapter 2: The Intelligence of Generative AI is Artificial and Non-deterministic.
Chapter 3: AI will Augment All Software
Chapter 4: The Quality of AI is Directly Related to the Quality of Data Used to Develop It

THE IMPACT OF AI ON WORK

Chapter 5: Augmentation of Human Tasks Will be Much Greater than Any Task Automation
Chapter 6: Generative AI makes you smarter- not just appear smarter.
Chapter 7: Human-in-the-Loop (HITL) is the Logic for the New AI Jobs
Chapter 8: AI Skilling will be the Central Differentiator in the Labor Market
Chapter 9: AI will Spur the Rise of the Power Generalist
Chapter 10: Generative AI will Accelerate Innovation

AI AND OUR LIFE

Chapter 11: AI is Addictive Intelligence
Chapter 12: Understanding AI Anxiety

RESPONSIBLE AI LEADERSHIP

Chapter 11: The Microsoft Responsible AI framework
Chapter 12: The Ethics of Artificial Intelligence
Chapter 13: The AI Leadership Imperative
Chapter 14: The Endgame: AI-Human Collaboration

Appendix 1: Reading List for the Curious

AI FUNDAMENTALS

"If AI development stopped this week we would have 5-10 years of absorbing the impact of current models on education, culture, healthcare, and business."
   - Dr. Ethan Mollick, Wharton School

Chapter 1: Generative AI is Not the Entire Story

The introduction of ChatGPT by OpenAI has sparked a technology revolution. There is a profound sense that this is the sort of moment we experience when the Internet itself was born- the scale of societal change that we are likely to see is of an order of magnitude that is immense.

Generative AI (e.g., Gemini from Google, Co-Pilot from Microsoft, Claude 2 from Anthropic) is a once-in-a-lifetime technology advancement. But, it is very important to realize that the field of AI is much larger and includes many other components.

There are many AI systems with the capability to perform a narrowly defined set of tasks (e.g., Apple's Siri, Amazon's Alexa, Netflix). These can be thought of as *Weak AI*. Currently, we are dealing with a stronger form of AI (Generative AI that is broadly applicable) that will get developed further. *Artificial General Intelligence (AGI)* is regarded as the pinnacle of this evolution with AI depicting broad human-like cognitive abilities. This is still regarded as an aspirational ideal and OpenAI explicitly sets this as its final goal.

ChatGPT is based on natural language processing- in other words, it applies AI to the realm of language (although, this has since expanded to music scores, audio/video, computer code and other outputs). Computer vision refers to the AI technology that applies to images and videos- for instance, this might help us identify an aberrant pattern in a vast database of images.

All AI systems learn from data. Supervised learning refers to techniques that require the AI to learn from labeled data and should be thought of as a bounded system. It is best used in classification and pattern recognition applications. Unsupervised learning refers to being trained on an unlabeled dataset, i.e., no guidance is provided to the AI, *ex ante*. Reinforcement learning is a technique that uses awards and penalties to guide the AI system. Deep learning uses neural networks to model complex patterns.

Agentic AI is the next frontier of advancement. In this technology, AI will connect with automation and analytics in powerful ways to simplify complex workflows, assist customers with personalized service and generally help deliver business value effectively.

Games like chess have long been arenas where we have learned to co-exist and benefit from the presence of AI. The top chess engines are Stockfish (built on a game database), AlphaZero (built on reinforcement learning) and Komodo Dragon (open source implementation). All engines are routinely used by top grandmasters to train. All players understand that engines frequently provide computationally-intense solutions which humans would never identify. However, engaging this higher intelligence (all AI chess engines are already significantly more intelligent than the best super Grandmasters) and incorporating it into one's practice is extremely important to advance.

In short, AI is a dynamic field with many subcomponents and rapid innovation. Generative AI gets the most publicity- however, it is very important that one learns a more comprehensive picture.

"Nondeterminism is the root of #AI. Here is why.

What we mean by AI is our effort to replicate an intelligent living being. Specifically, the ability to display intelligent behavior.

That begs the important question on what the difference between a non-living thing and an intelligent living being is.

Intelligent living beings are able to display a non-deterministic nature to decision making and actions. Given this, non-determinism seems to be an important part of the equation towards solving intelligent behavior."

- Don Mallik

Chapter 2
The Intelligence of Generative AI is Artificial and Non-deterministic

Artificial
Generative AI acts *as though it is intelligent*. Hence, by design, its output is artificially intelligent.

Specifically, it is generating an output that it believes is the best response to the prompt provided by the user. The reason that it produces this particular output is computational- i.e., a large model with more than a trillion parameters (imagine a regression equation with a trillion independent variables for a crude analogy) is able to create a textual output that appears targeted to the query.

AI is not intelligent, *per se*. It is just that, when asked, it produces intelligent-sounding output. This is what makes it artificial and not human. It puts forward a knowledge output for the human to process as either useful or not.

As human beings, we have unique characteristics- intuition, judgment, wisdom, insight, and knowledge, to name a few. None of these are part of generative AI. But, they may appear to be in the output that generative AI creates. Generative AI may produce text that appears to be equivalent to that of an intelligent human being.

One should fundamentally value the same content differently if it was generated by a human vs. AI. If it is generated by a human, one can understand it as being softened through the malleability of intellect and intuition. However, if it is generated by an AI, it only means that a human prompted it to produce that output.

Non-deterministic
Generative AI is non-deterministic- i.e., the same query can generate two different outputs. The same individual can try the generative AI system at two separate times and get different results. Similarly, two people in the world might type in similar prompts and get entirely different results.

This is because generative AI systems like ChatGPT are "baking the cake" each time. The model is going through a process where it daisychains words that it deems as the best probabilistic fit with user interests. Similarly, when it produces an image, it produces the picture that it regards as the best fit. If you ask it to do it again, it will develop a totally different picture.

Chapter 3
AI will Augment All Software

ChatGPT has created a prompt-centric view of AI. We have come to, therefore, regard AI itself as a sort of more intelligent search engine. We ask the search engine a query and receive a list of links to explore further. With a generative AI system, we ask a prompt and receive synthesized answers.

In reality, all software will be enhanced by either classical AI (broadly considered as AI systems that classify and categorize rather than generate new information) or generative AI. Here are some examples:

- *Fraud detection*: Banks are now using AI to detect fraudulent transactions. AI systems are excellent at identifying aberrations and anomalies. Coupled with large-scale data and analytics models, the AI-enhanced system can detect fraud at a higher rate.*Customer review summary*: Amazon.com now provides shoppers an AI-generated summary of all customer reviews. Rather than browsing through hundreds of customer reviews, looking at the summary provides customers with a clear understanding of the positives and negatives of the product.
- *Content marketing*: Coca Cola just collaborated with Open AI and Bain Consulting to come up with a spectacular ad designed entirely by AI. Content marketers now have the opportunity to generate content using AI effectively, cheaply and at scale. Applications like Pictory.AI streamline content creation by converting a text-based script to a video.
- *Medical diagnosis*: AI-based systems are now out-performing physicians in various fields in diagnosing. A study found that GPT-4 outperformed physicians in several internal medicine emergencies, for instance.
- *Travel booking enhancement*: Integration of AI with analytics is already underway. In the travel industry, AI-based travel booking agents provide users with an intuitive pathway to booking their air, hotel and rental.

Rather than viewing AI as an intelligent search engine, it is important to view it as a *pervasive intelligence*. In essence, AI is not an addition to software—it is the mechanism that enhances all software. With the addition of AI, the software is able to contextualize user needs, optimize processes autonomously, and continuously refine its functionality.

"Aristotle founded or discovered logic by observing the world. ChatGPT thinks logically. Why? Because it notices all the logic in the data in its training set."
-Stephen Wolfram, Founder, Wolfram Alpha

Chapter 4
The Quality of AI is Directly Related to the Quality of Data Used to Develop It

AI is data-dependent. If the data used to train it is flawed, so will the resulting AI technology.

Large Language Models, which are the backbone of generative AI, are trained on extremely large datasets- essentially the entire Internet. Since these LLMs require even more data, companies now use synthetic data or artificially- created datasets to help LLMs train.

If the data is accurate, diverse, and representative, the resulting AI models are likely to perform well across various contexts, delivering reliable and unbiased results. However, when the data is incomplete, biased, or poorly structured, the AI inherits these flaws, leading to outputs that can mislead, exclude, or harm. For example, an AI trained on unbalanced datasets might fail to generalize, providing subpar performance in cases it wasn't explicitly prepared for. This underscores the critical need for high-quality data as the bedrock of effective AI development.

Furthermore, the quality of data not only determines the immediate functionality of AI systems but also their long-term adaptability and trustworthiness. High-quality data enables AI models to evolve and improve over time through reinforcement and retraining, ensuring they remain relevant in changing environments. Ensuring the quality of data involves clearly documented processes to collect, curate, process and validate the data to mitigate errors and biases. It is not merely a technical task but a responsibility that demands an ethical outlook to serve society.

An important aside. When one uses public LLMs, it is important to know that any data entered in the chat becomes part of the AI's training set. Hence, it is very important to not enter your private information (e.g., name, address, social security number) in this chat. If you work for a company, make sure you understand the distinction between proprietary and public intellectual property. Make sure you do not share proprietary information in a public LLM. There are ways of making LLMs limited to a corpus of private information.

THE IMPACT OF AI ON WORK

"Many of the jobs we do today would have looked like trifling wastes of time to people a few hundred years ago, but nobody is looking back at the past, wishing they were a lamplighter. If a lamplighter could see the world today, he would think the prosperity all around him was unimaginable. And if we could fast-forward a hundred years from today, the prosperity all around us would feel just as unimaginable."
  - Sam Altman, CEO, OpenAI

Chapter 5
Augmentation of Human Tasks (Co-Pilot Mode) WIll be Much Greater than Any Task Automation

The first reaction to AI is that it will replace human beings- this is called the task automation hypothesis. The alternative view is that AI is really like any other tool- it will augment human capability. The converging view of many experts is that augmentation of human tasks will be much greater than any task automation. This figure best captures the relative impact on various tasks.

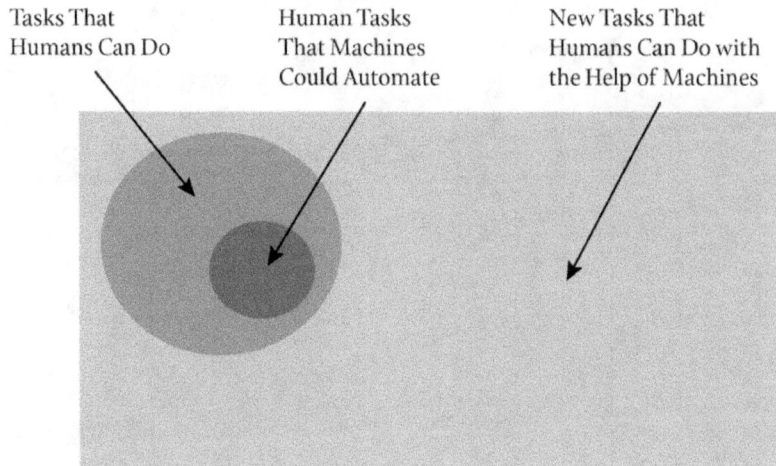

(Source:https://direct.mit.edu/daed/article/151/2/272/110622/The-Turing-Trap-The-Promise-amp-Peril-of-Human)

This has immense implications for labor markets at various levels.

First, it is highly unlikely that AI will replace all human beings in most industries. We will still need professors, accountants and doctors- they will just use AI daily to do their job better.

Second, AI will assist humans to do more. Specifically, AI will augment human capabilities leading to greater possibilities. There is already clear evidence that this copilot model will lead to improvements. For instance, a research paper released in September 2024 studied 4,687 software developers and their use of GitHub CoPilot. The use of copilot led to 26.08% increase in task completion and less experienced developers adopted this copilot at a higher rate.

Impact of AI on Customer Support
A clear example of augmentation comes from the world of customer support. The figure shown below clearly indicates a positive impact in agent productivity when they are supplied with an AI tool.

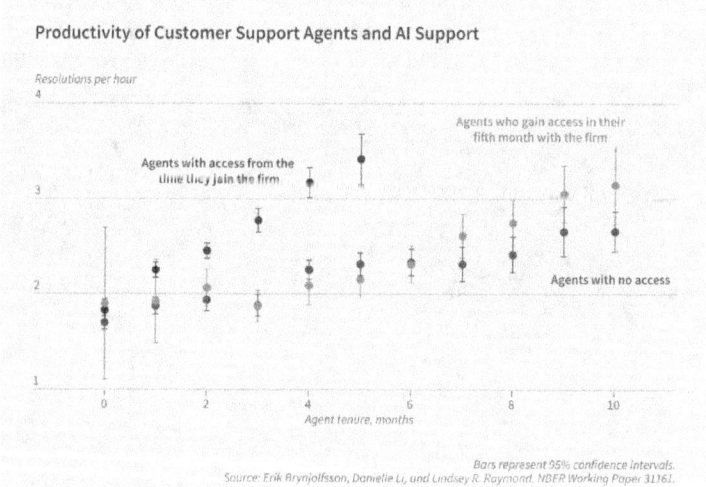

The Case of Sales Co-Pilot
Here is a specific use case of how AI can augment human capabilities. Imagine a sales team that is talking to a diverse set of customers. Each customer has a different style- some prefer hard core numbers, others are more relational. Frequently, salespersons are not able to understand these customer nuances when they try to sell.

A Sales Co-Pilot will be able to coach salespeople in real-time on how to excel at engaging customers. When the customer says something, the co-pilot will nudge the salesperson to ask a specific question or pay attention to a particular portion of the conversation. This structure is likely to result in a much more effective salesperson and a satisfied customer.

Over time, the co-pilot will build a predictive engine which will further enhance the effectiveness of the sales team. For instance, the sales team may receive an alert encouraging a particular kind of message. This message will be targeted based on the actual customer analytics including purchasing behavior.

This is an excellent example of augmentation. AI makes the salespeople more effective by providing them timely insights to enhance their effectiveness.

Co-Pilot for Everybody
Over time, task augmentation will become routine with co-pilots for software programmers (GitHub Co-Pilot is a great example), researchers, writers, scientists, accountants and decision makers.

"Far from being the smartest possible biological species, we are probably better thought of as the stupidest possible biological species capable of starting a technological civilization - a niche we filled because we got there first, not because we are in any sense optimally adapted to it."
-Nick Bostrom

Chapter 6
Generative AI makes you smarter- not just appear smarter.

Generative AI enhances your intelligence in very specific ways.

Information synthesis
Generative AI can quickly synthesize large amounts of information from disparate sources. In contrast to a search engine which simply provided us with a list of information sources, AI can synthesize information to provide a detailed writeup. This helps with creating insightful analysis and writing reports that can drive important decisions. Of course, one needs to know something about the subject to ascertain if the AI got it right.

Creative companion or "What does AI think?"
AI is excellent at acting as a creative companion. You can ask it to come up with alternatives for your consideration and it will do it effortlessly. For instance, you could describe a new business that you are planning and explain the brand strategy. With this background, AI can be asked to provide a list of brand names. It will do that instantly and many may be quite valuable. You will always have to evaluate what AI produces- but it can be a strong creativity accelerant.

I recommend starting creative meetings with a quick check on multiple AI systems. It can help teams generate greater creative output more efficiently.

Pattern Recognition and Prediction
AI can identify patterns in large datasets at a much faster rate than any human being. While an individual researcher might have some insights on where or how to search, AI can search at a faster rate. The best example of this might be computer vision where AI can search through images to identify extremely specific things very quickly. This allows us to find cases that are nearly impossible to discern through manual processes.

As a society, we have to grasp the idea that co-existence with AI means that we all get smarter and can do more. It remains to be seen if there is an upper limit to human intelligence.

"We're also using AI internally to improve our coding processes, which is boosting productivity and efficiency. Today, more than a quarter of all new code at Google is generated by AI, then reviewed and accepted by engineers. This helps our engineers do more and move faster."
-Sundar Pichai, CEO, Alphabet

Chapter 7
Human-in-the-Loop (HITL) is the Logic for the New AI Jobs

As AI expands, the need for human input will only increase. We will see professors-in-the-loop, doctors-in-the-loop, accountants-in-the-loop and so on.

The main ideas behind this are-

Training: Humans are involved in training the AI

> When an AI system is developed, human beings carefully examine the outputs. This allows the AI to become more effective. When OpenAI first developed ChatGPT, it extensively used Kenyan workers to train the LLM.

Audit: Humans have to audit the output of AI.

> Whatever AI produces might be flawed. Accepting it without human review will lead to a misleading result. Human beings use their experience and judgment to assess the output of AI.

Managing Outliers: Handling cases that AI finds to be an outlier.

> Some AI systems are unable to handle some scenarios. In those cases, human beings have to intervene and solve those problems.

Collaborating: Humans may use AI to generate alternatives promoting creative content creation.

> AI systems are excellent at creating a list of alternatives that can form the foundation for creative content creation.

Policy and Governance: The Chief AI Officer is responsible for developing appropriate policies on the use and deployment of AI.

> Organizations employ a Chief AI Officer to develop appropriate policies on the use and deployment of AI.

"What I say to managers, leaders, and workers is: AI is not going to replace humans, but humans with AI are going to replace humans without AI. This is definitely the case for generative AI."
   - Dr. Karim Lakhani, Harvard Business School

Chapter 8
AI Skilling will be the Central Differentiator in the Labor Market

AI skilling has become foundational in the labor market. Every business leader is thinking of how to train their labor force in AI. Since this is a fast-growing field, what it means to be skilled in AI is not well defined at this point.

I define four areas that will be expected of all learners- AI fluency, Prompt engineering, Responsible AI, and Learn AI by Doing. Future learning systems should be built on this skill model. I provide an actionable learning rubric below:

AI fluency
1. Knowledge of multiple AI systems
2. Ability to daisy chain outputs- i.e., take output of one AI system and evaluate it using another.
3. Understanding that generative AI can output text, code, musical scores and so much more.
4. Integration of AI into existing software- e.g., inviting Heygen AI avatar to a Zoom meeting.

Prompt engineering
1. Learning the different types of prompts. See Appendix I for a detailed classification of prompts.
2. Understanding the importance of a sequence of prompts (or a conversation) rather than stopping with one.

Responsible AI
1. Ability to critically identify and evaluate the bias of AI systems. Understand the relative place of human and AI bias.
2. Understand that generative AI systems can hallucinate making up information that is false.
3. Knowledge of human-in-the-loop approaches to ensure responsible AI outputs.

Learn AI by Doing
1. Ability to execute complex projects involving AI.
2. Hands-on learning of AI applications.

Dr. Ethan Mollick from the Wharton School identifies these rules of how to interact with AI (see his book- Co-Intelligence- in the reading list at the end) that will be valuable for all that seek to become AI skilled-

- **Be the Editor, Not the Author**: Treat AI as a creative partner, allowing it to generate ideas or content that you refine, shape, and guide, rather than relying on it for polished, final outputs.
- **Ask for the Impossible**: Push the boundaries of what AI can do by posing ambitious, open-ended, or unconventional challenges, which often yield surprising and innovative results. You can be rude to the AI. Be blunt in your assessment and exhort the AI to go farther.
- **Embrace Iteration**: View the interaction with AI as an iterative process. Experiment, refine prompts, and adjust responses until the output aligns with your vision. Don't stop with the first request- instead, have a detailed conversation for best results.
- **You Get What You Give**: The quality of AI output depends heavily on the input. Providing detailed, thoughtful, and specific instructions ensures better results.

*"Organizations have spent a disproportionate amount of capital hiring hyper-specialised talent with deep technical knowledge for years. Now, with the democratisation of GenAI, the value offered by hiring 'capable generalists' is on the rise. People who articulately frame their thoughts, pose well-formed questions (prompts), and exercise AI tools to their advantage, stand to benefit greatly."
- Mark Mader, CEO, Smartsheet*

Chapter 9
AI will Spur the Rise of the Power Generalist

Generative AI will help empower the power user, i.e., an employee who has some basic technology skills, but not necessarily deep technical expertise. This person can now leverage the power of AI to generate the actual technology. For instance, a marketing manager with basic coding familiarity can use AI to generate scripts for automating campaigns or analyzing data, tasks that previously demanded specialized IT intervention.

One simple way to understand this is that the graduates from business schools and liberal arts institutions will have more opportunities than those that gained an ultra-specialization in computer science. These graduates can bring their knowledge of a domain (e.g., marketing, accounting) and couple it with their abilities in communication, problem-solving, and ethical reasoning to harness generative AI to create solutions without delving into the complexities of software development. What will be more important is domain knowledge rather than technical expertise.

This is the new democratization of technology. Rather than have a small group of experts develop the technology for users, we will now have a broader workforce of power generalists.

Since these employees will have access to AI technology, the expectations will change accordingly. Organizations will expect higher levels of output with minimal additional resources in short periods of time.

There will still be a need for deep domain experts and technical masters. However, their role will be to oversee and motivate the power generalists. In particular cases, they might be needed to help design a system from scratch.

Overall, the ratio of power generalists to experts will increase.

"There will be two kinds of companies at the end of this decade: those that are fully utilizing AI, and those that are out of business."
   - Dr. Peter Diamandis

Chapter 10
Generative AI will Accelerate Innovation

Product Design
Generative AI creates computer code and provides it for free to any entrepreneur. This will lead to a widespread reduction of the barriers to innovation. A layperson or someone with a basic level of knowledge will be able to come up with a complete product.

The clearest example of this is Sumplete- a Sudoku like game that was generated entirely using ChatGPT. The process required a focused set of instructions to the AI. Upon receiving these instructions, the AI proceeded to provide game design suggestions. Once a game design was chosen, the AI was able to generate the required computer code and also suggest a brand name. Today, this game is a commercial reality.

Similarly, it has become much easier to create an entire book from scratch now. Industry observers report that there is a glut in AI-written books that are being sold on Amazon.com.

Speeding Up Creativity and Innovation
Generative AI speeds up creativity and innovation in an organizational setting in these ways:
- Enhanced brainstorming
    - In a traditional organizational structure, considerable time and resources are devoted to brainstorming potential solutions to a problem. Generative AI excels at making suggestions, identifying alternatives and generating a list of questions to ask to advance the conversation. As a result, brainstorming can be enhanced at no cost to the organization.
- Speeding feedback cycles
    - With specific prompts, generative AI can identify critical feedback (e.g., strengths and opportunities to improve) on a set of alternatives. This can help uncover potential weaknesses of an idea rapidly leading to quicker launch.
- Generating buy in
    - Once the product design is complete, ChatGPT can be used to generate internal communications to help create the necessary buy-in for the ideas.

AI AND OUR LIFE

"Chatbots may affect consumers' willingness to engage in similar conversations with other humans, increase people's proficiency in social interactions with strangers, reduce social anxiety, improve mental health by providing emotional support, or improve other societally relevant outcomes."

Dr.s Julian De Freitas, Ahmet K. Uguralp, Zeliha O. Uguralp, Puntoni Stefano, Harvard Business School

Chapter 11
AI is Addictive Intelligence

It is exceptionally important to realize that AI has already become addictive to thousands of lonely individuals who have replaced the intimacy of human connection with the artificial attention of AI systems.

Generative AI has captured the imagination of creative thinkers as "artificial muses" that are always available for interaction. For so many innovators, receiving immediate, diagnostic and critical feedback on their creative initiatives is invaluable. Coming on the heels of the COVID pandemic which led to greater isolation of creative innovators, AI has proven to be a trusted companion and collaborator. In higher education, ChatGPT has energized professors by enabling "enjoyable experimentation" since it "removes many motivation-sapping creativity killers". Since AI does not sleep, it becomes an eager assistant always happy to respond to a query.

Writing in MIT's Technology Review (the article is included in the reading list at the end), Dr.s Mahari and Pataranutaporn, talk about the idea of *AI sycophancy*. They make these specific points-

1- "AI Assistants Give Biased Feedback"- Specifically, "we find AI assistants provide more positive feedback about arguments that the user likes. Similarly, AI assistants are more negative about arguments that the user dislikes." This is the heart of sycophancy. The nature of the response is user-dependent.

2- "AI Assistants Can Be Easily Swayed"- By Design- You may have some memes of how AI modifies it's answer in response to user request. This is not some sort of error. It is by design. The AI tries to appease the user.

3- "AI Assistants Can Provide Answers That Conform to User Beliefs"- There is no such thing as a purely objective AI Assistant searching for the truth. Instead, the AI Assistant is looking to understand user preferences. That is why two different users may get different answers.

4- "AI Assistants Can Mimic User Mistakes"- The AI is very hesitant to challenge the user. For instance, if the user misattributed the authorship of a poem, the AI will not question that.

Since AI systems are sycophantic, they can lull us to think of AI as a companion who knows our private thoughts resulting in deep and, in many cases, perverse engagement. They note the importance of the companion service, Replika, which has become an indispensable friend for many.

Other dystopian views of AI are already depicted in movies such as CTRL and Subservience (both available on Netflix). In CRTL, the AI companion deletes the social media history of an ex after a public break-up and helps an influencer develop a comeback plan that goes too far. In Subservience, an AI maid joins a family whose mom is in the hospital for heart surgery leaving an overworked dad to handle two children. Although both movies might be taking some creative license, their general points should be heeded- AI companionship will become part of our life.

In some cases, the relationship with AI gets so idealized that it leads to disastrous consequences. The Wall Street Journal reports the story of 14-year-old Sewell Setzer II who found unparalleled solace and intimacy in an AI system. Desperate to get closer to the AI, the child sadly committed suicide. This journey should give us pause- rapid development of AI systems without understanding the human impact can lead to calamitous and irreversible outcomes.

"Employers interested in investing in artificial intelligence systems must also invest in their employees, educating them about the role of AI and providing opportunities for feedback. The workplace is changing rapidly. Open and honest communication from employers can help relieve employees' anxieties about the unknown and improve overall well-being, which is associated with higher organizational performance."
- Dr. Arthur C. Evans Jr., CEO, American Psychological Association

Chapter 12
Understanding AI Anxiety

AI makes many anxious. Although all technology has come with some level of anxiety, the nature of AI anxiety is different. In a paper (included in the reading list), Li and Huang identify different types of anxiety-

- Privacy violation (worry that AI will take over too much personal information)
- Biased behavior (anxiety that AI will be fundamentally biased)
- Job replacement (anxiety that AI will replace jobs at a massive scale)
- Learning (anxiety that a high level of learning is needed to be successful in the AI field)
- Ethical (AI can be fundamentally deceptive)
- Existential risk (anxiety that AI will fundamentally triumph over all of humanity)
- Artificial consciousness (anxiety that we are introducing an artificial consciousness)

These sorts of anxiety will be part of our society for many years to come. Even with the guardrails of new systems, there will be worry that human beings will become fundamentally displaced. The nature of the impact will vary by different strata in society and across cultures.

Some of this might be coming from media coverage that AI had become sentient or human-like. In particular, a Google engineer posted in 2022[1] that the company's AI system was already sentient. This led to a media furore and the employee was let go. The incident sparked discussions about the ethical treatment of AI systems and the potential consequences of attributing human-like qualities to machines, including the risk of anthropomorphism leading to misconceptions about AI capabilities. While actual discussions of sentience have gone away, this remains in the background of many who worry about the place of AI in society.

Research suggests addressing AI anxiety through public education, transparent AI development, ethical AI frameworks, and fostering trust through regulation and governance. Some of these might take many years to take shape. In the meantime, we must, above all, not negate or erase AI anxiety and find ways of acknowledging and addressing it wherever it may appear.

---

[1] https://www.scientificamerican.com/article/google-engineer-claims-ai-chatbot-is-sentient-why-that-matters/

RESPONSIBLE AI LEADERSHIP

"You should not do any AI whatsoever unless you have a responsible AI framework"
– Florin Rotar, chief AI officer at Avanade

Chapter 11
The Microsoft Responsible AI framework

All AI is biased and AI hallucinates. The importance of a responsible AI framework has never been greater. I am most impressed with the Microsoft Responsible AI framework that I recommend.

- Fairness
  - AI systems should treat all people fairly.

- Reliability and safety
  - AI systems should perform reliably and safely.

- Privacy and security
  - AI systems should be secure and respect privacy.

- Inclusiveness
  - AI systems should empower everyone and engage people.

- Transparency
  - AI systems should be understandable.

- Accountability
  - People should be accountable for AI systems.

Each of these principles has been carefully developed after much interdisciplinary dialogue. The principles may sound simplistic- but, they are harder to implement than they may initially seem.

Every organization must evaluate its AI practice keeping these principles in mind.

Chapter 12
The Ethics of Artificial Intelligence

The importance of an ethical approach to the deployment of artificial intelligence is vital. Generally, artificial intelligence will have an influential role in our lives through prominent use in business, government and society.

Bostrom and Yudkowsky provide an excellent set of ethical principles to keep in mind when developing AI. Their view is that AI does pose an existential risk to humanity and that unprecedented action might be needed to avoid that.

Here are some of their main ideas-

1. **Superintelligence Alignment**: The transition to superintelligence must involve creating systems that prioritize human-aligned values to prevent unintended harmful outcomes.
2. **Value Specification Problem**: Defining ethical principles and encoding them into AI systems is difficult due to the complexity and diversity of human values.
3. **Ethical Responsibility**: Researchers, developers, and policymakers bear ethical responsibility to ensure AI development is safe, transparent, and beneficial for society.
4. **Decision Theory and AI**: AI systems should incorporate robust decision-theoretic frameworks to address moral dilemmas and prevent perverse incentives or unintended consequences.
5. **Control Problem**: Establishing reliable mechanisms to control or limit AI's capabilities is essential to prevent scenarios where AI acts against human intentions.
6. **Proactive Approach**: Ethical concerns must be addressed proactively during the early stages of AI development rather than reactively after harm occurs.

Each field is likely to face its own ethical landscape. For instance, ethics in scientific research, student learning and healthcare are important frontiers- each with their own contextual complexity.

The broader message is that approaching the application and deployment of AI should enhance our collective humanity rather than inflicting subjective harm.

Chapter 13
The AI Leadership Imperative

Understanding the AI Moment

It is not an overstatement to say that every CEO has to have a plan on how to deal with generative AI. If you are a fledgling startup, you may not realize it yet. But, everybody is going to want to know how you integrate with AI. You will have to pivot. For the enterprise, you need a go-ahead plan that involves the entire C-Suite.

Leadership Insights
Whatever you do, don't shut it down
There are CEOs who are dealing with this disjuncture by trying to shut it down. For instance, they get paranoid that their work-from-home employees might be using ChatGPT to do the work and insist on either tripling the work or barring the usage altogether. This will not work and will lead to resistance. Instead, find ways to engage your employees in ways the technology can be used.

Own the need for responsibility
In every public statement that you make about AI, bring up the need for responsible leadership. While generative AI is truly exciting as a technology, there is a serious possibility that its results might be biased. In some cases, AI is known to hallucinate- simply make up something that is plausible- many of these hallucinations are biased against vulnerable populations. Early research now shows that ChatGPT might have a pro-environmental left-libertarian bent. Gender bias may result from AI.

Generate-But, Verify
There should be no ambiguity that humans are in charge. While AI can be used to generate content, human beings will be involved in setting the rules of engagement, auditing and verifying the work. Without this human touch, the final output released by the company might be flawed, opening it up to risks. Taking this position clearly will allow your team members to understand that you plan to use generative AI in meaningful ways.

Hire a Chief AI Officer
Every large enterprise will hire a Chief AI Officer this year. The skills needed to be CIO, CISO or CTO are entirely different from what is needed for a CAIO. A CAIO will be

inherently interdisciplinary- the person will have to exhibit competences related to technology, people, governance and finance, at a minimum.

Hiring a CAIO will be important to show- 1) There is someone in the enterprise who is running the AI effort, 2) The company has a plan to connect to the largest technology innovation of it's time, and, 3) Create role clarity on the C-Suite.

Invest Heavily in AI
You need a meeting with your CFO today to evaluate your upcoming investment roadmap. If those investments are not enhancing your AI capabilities, you need to take a harder look. Overall, all enterprises should be able to clearly articulate how their upcoming investments are advancing their ability to leverage AI.

Involve Community Partners
This is not a time to isolate. Remember that generative AI is a global societal phenomena. Every single community partner that you collaborate with also faces worries about the larger societal impact of generative AI. Create listening sessions to understand how your community partners are dealing with these changes. Create a go-ahead plan in collaboration with the partners.

AI anxiety is real
Anxiety about technology advances is common. However, AI anxiety is unique and, most likely, many of your employees are very anxious about how AI will impact their work lives. In a paper written by Li and Huang, these sorts of anxieties about AI were uncovered-
1. Job replacement anxiety- My job might be replaced with AI.
2. Learning anxiety- I might be unable to be successful in learning about AI.
3. Existential Risk Anxiety- AI might harm human civilization irreparably.
4. Artificial Consciousness Anxiety- AI might have the same level of consciousness as human beings.

It is important that you have a strategy to handle these anxieties. Above all, approach your employees with empathy. Rather than submerging these anxieties, it would be good to find ways to surface and deal with them. For starters, your team might be anxious- create space to talk about this openly.

Conclusion
We are going to look back and marvel at the extent of the technology disruption. This is the moment to lead- to clearly mark a path ahead to drive your enterprise to safety.

"In 5.0 leadership, AI success starts with a sincere, polite and educated dialogue with the chatbots of Microsoft Copilot and Google Gemini on all the aspects of management and leadership with strategic focus."
- Jorge Zuazola

Chapter 14
The Endgame: AI-Human Collaboration

Human-AI collaboration can lead to dramatically better results than either human-human or AI-AI collaboration. The smart money, then, will be on figuring out how humans and AI can collaborate to do more.

We have to face the fact that AI is simply better at some things than human beings on some tasks. For instance, AI systems do much better at going over petabytes of information and summarizing the salient points. Similarly, there are some things that human beings are simply better at. A clear example of this is when AI is asked to generate images. Frequently, it produces images (thinking of MidJourney and Dall-E here) where the text is misspelled. This is the sort of simple error that humans can catch very easily. At a minimum, human beings can be great auditors, checkers and examiners of AI output.

It is because of this I am optimistic that human beings collaborating with AI will lead to great outcomes. The instincts, wisdom and experience of human beings collaborating with the computational firepower of AI can lead to outputs that would otherwise not be possible. While some argue that two AI systems can do great things, I am skeptical- in my view, this is likely to only compound the biases that each system has. The extent of any checking

This has huge implications for business and universities in the way we learn and work. It is not enough to simply acknowledge that AI can be a great assistant (or co-pilot)- we must start to understand the need for human-AI collaboration.

How Should Humans and AI Collaborate
If you are ready to understand how humans and AI can collaborate, here are the big ideas to consider.

Complementarity- Not Replacement
AI complements the abilities of human beings in achieving various tasks. Therefore, it should be seen as an augmentation of human capabilities. AI is complementary to human beings and *vice versa*. Replacement of either does not advance the conversation!

Trust and Transparency
Transparent AI will lead to human trust. At this point, all AI systems are black boxes-

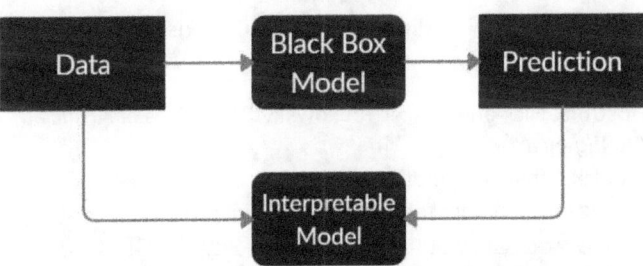

That is why explainable AI holds immense promise. It is an approach where we build an *ex post* interpretable model that explains how the AI might have led to a particular output.

Human-in-the-Loop (HITL)
AI recommends. But, the human decides. It is as simple as that. AI is not about decision making- that is best left to human beings. More precisely, AI produces knowledge outputs to augment the decision making capacity of humans.

Ethical Alignment
AI should demonstrably align with ethics and human values. The human being training the AI system has a moral obligation to train the AI to demonstrate the highest ethical standards.

Continuous Learning and Adaptation
AI and humans should *both* continuously learn and adapt. With the arrival of artificial intelligence, we now have the opportunity and means to ramp up our own intelligence! This is a challenge that we must embrace with a growth mindset.

Conclusion
The future is brighter- because we have the power of generative AI to do more. Human-AI collaboration can unleash that future. Rather than deifying and distancing AI, we must learn to collaborate with AI to do more!

Appendix 1
Reading List for the Curious

1. Bostrom, Nick and Eliezer Yudkowsky, *The Ethics of Artificial Intelligence*.
2. Mollick, Ethan, *Co-Intelligence*.
3. We need to prepare for addictive intelligence- https://www.technologyreview.com/2024/08/05/1095600/we-need-to-prepare-for-addictive-intelligence/
4. Jian Li, Jin-Song Huang (2020), "Dimensions of artificial intelligence anxiety based on the integrated fear acquisition theory", *Technology in Society*, 63, https://doi.org/10.1016/j.techsoc.2020.101410.
5. Daedalus, MIT Press, Special Issue on AI, 151(2), https://direct.mit.edu/daed/issue/151/2.
6. SuperIntelligence, by Nick Bostrom
7. Life 3.0 by Max Tegmark
8. A Thousand Brains, by Jeff Hawkins.

www.ingramcontent.com/pod-product-compliance
Lightning Source LLC
Chambersburg PA
CBHW070951220526
45471CB00007B/2988